2
College Vocabulary

ENGLISH FOR ACADEMIC SUCCESS

Chaudron Gille
Gainesville College

SERIES EDITORS

Patricia Byrd

Joy M. Reid

Cynthia M. Schuemann

THOMSON
™
HEINLE

Australia • Canada • Mexico • Singapore • Spain • United Kingdom • United States

College Vocabulary 2
English for Academic Sucess
Chaudron Gille

Publisher: Patricia A. Coryell
Director of ESL Publishing: Susan Maguire
Senior Development Editor: Kathleen Sands-Boehmer
Editorial Assistant: Evangeline Bermas

Senior Project Editor: Kathryn Dinovo
Manufacturing Assistant: Karmen Chong
Senior Marketing Manager: Annamarie Rice

For permission to use material from this text or product, submit a request online at http://www.thomsonrights.com

Any additional questions about permissions can be submitted by email to thomsonrights@thomson.com

Printed in the United States of America.
4   5   6   7   8   9   10   09   08

Library of Congress Control Number: 2004112190

ISBN 10: 0-618-23025-4
ISBN 13: 978-0-618-23025-9

For more information contact Thomson Heinle, 25 Thomson Place, Boston, MA 02210 USA, or visit our Internet site at elt.heinle.com

Cover graphics: © LMA Communications, Natick, Massachusetts

Contents

English for Academic Success Series

▷ What Is the Vocabulary Strand All About?

The English for Academic Success series is a comprehensive program of student and instructor materials. There are four levels of student language proficiency textbooks in three skill areas (oral communication, reading, and writing) and a supplemental vocabulary textbook at each level. Knowing how to learn and use academic vocabulary is a fundamental skill for college students. Even students with fluency in conversational English need to become effective at learning academic words for their college courses. All of the textbooks in the English for Academic Success (EAS) series include work on vocabulary as part of academic reading, academic writing, and academic oral communication. In addition, this series provides four Vocabulary textbooks that focus on expanding student academic vocabulary and their skills as vocabulary learners. These textbooks can be used alone or can be combined with a reading, writing, or oral communication textbook. When used with one of the textbooks in the English for Academic Success series, the vocabulary textbooks can be provided at a reduced cost and shrink-wrapped with the reading, writing, or oral communication books.

Academic vocabulary involves two kinds of words: (1) general academic vocabulary that is used in many different disciplines, and (2) highly technical words that are limited to a particular field of study. As they prepare for academic study, students need first to learn generally used academic words. A list of the general academic words called the Academic Word List (AWL) has been published by Averil Coxhead.[1] Coxhead organizes AWLs words into lists based on word families, defining a *word family* as a set of related words.

The Vocabulary textbooks prepare students for their academic study by teaching them the meanings and uses of the AWL words. The AWL word families are divided among the four textbooks with each book presenting approximately 143 word families. To see the word lists for each book, visit the website for the vocabulary series at elt.heinle.com/collegevocab.

Learning new words is more effective when words are studied in meaningful contexts. Each chapter in the Vocabulary series contextualizes a set of approximately 25–30 AWL words in a "carrier topic" of interest to students. The carrier topics are intended to make the study more interesting as well as to provide realistic contexts for the words being studied. Learning a new word means learning its meaning, pronunciation, spelling, uses, and related members of the word's family. To help students with these learning challenges, the Vocabulary textbooks provide multiple encounters with words in a wide variety of activity types.

---

1. The AWL was introduced to the TESL/TEFL world with Coxhead's *TESOL Quarterly* publication: Coxhead, A. (2000). A new academic word list. *TESOL Quarterly 34*(2); 213–238. Coxhead is also the author of the *Essentials of Teaching Academic Vocabulary*, a teacher-reference book in the English for Academic Success series.

Each chapter has been structured to incorporate learning strategies or tips that will help students become active acquirers and collectors of words. Additionally, because research supports the idea that multiple exposures are of great significance in learning vocabulary, each word family is practiced repeatedly and many are recycled in the lessons and chapters that follow their introduction. Newly introduced vocabulary appears in **bold** type. Recycled vocabulary is indicated by a dotted underline.

Student websites for the Vocabulary textbooks provide additional practice with the AWL words as well as useful review chapters. Instructors and students can download these review chapters for use as homework or in-class study. The website for each book expands the practice with the AWL words covered in that book. Students can access vocabulary flash cards for the complete 570 word families if they choose to work with words beyond those introduced in the particular vocabulary textbook they are studying. Each of these flash cards has the AWL word, its definition, and an example.

Although, with the addition of online answer keys, this book can be an aid to self-study, it is ideally suited for classroom use. According to the focus of your course, you may choose to have your students respond to some of the exercises in writing, while you may choose to make oral activities of others. Of course, you can also incorporate practice in both skills by following oral discussion with a writing assignment. You may ask students to work individually on some exercises, while others will be better suited to pair or small-group configurations.

Acknowledgments

This book is the result of the efforts and support of a wonderful group of people. I would first like to thank Susan Maguire, Houghton Mifflin Director of ESL Publishing, and Kathy Sands Boehmer, Houghton Mifflin ESL Development Editor, for their belief in and support of this series. I would also like to thank the series editors Cynthia Schuemann, Joy Reid, and especially Patricia Byrd, whose encouragement and guidance kept me on track. I would like to thank my fellow vocabulary series authors, John Bunting, Keith Folse, Marcella Farina, and Julie Howard, for their experience, ideas, and friendship.

I would also like to thank my advisors, Tonna Harris-Boselman, Jane Lineberger, and Jeanne White for their invaluable advice and feedback.

Finally, I would like to thank my family and friends for their encouragement and love.

◢ What Student Competencies Are Covered in *College Vocabulary 1–4?*

Description of Overall Purposes

Students develop the ability to understand and use words from the Academic Word List (AWL) that are frequently encountered in college course work.

Materials in this textbook are designed with the following minimum exit objectives in mind:

Competency 1:   The student will recognize the meaning of selected academic vocabulary words.

Competency 2:   The student will demonstrate controlled knowledge of the meaning of selected academic vocabulary words.

Competency 3:   The student will demonstrate active use of selected academic vocabulary words.

Competency 4:   The student will develop and apply strategies for vocabulary learning. The student will:
   a. recognize roots, affixes, and inflected forms.
   b. distinguish among members of word families.
   c. identify and interpret word functions.
   d. recognize and manipulate appropriate collocations.
   e. use contextual clues to aid understanding.
   f. develop word learning resources such as flash cards and personal lists.
   g. increase awareness of how words are recycled in written text and oral communication.
   h. increase awareness of the benefits of rehearsal for word learning (repetition and reuse of words in multiple contexts).

Competency 5:   The student will use dictionaries for vocabulary development and to distinguish among multiple meanings of a word.

Competency 6:   The student will analyze words for syllable and stress patterns and use such analysis to aid in correct pronunciation.

Competency 7:   The student will analyze words for spelling patterns.

Competency 8:   The student will become familiar with web-based resources for learning AWL words.

Money Matters

In this chapter, you will

- ► Become familiar with twenty-three words that are useful in academic English
- ► Learn to identify some common **suffixes** and **prefixes**
- ► Use **antonyms** and **synonyms** to help you learn new vocabulary
- ► Learn more about **word families**
- ► Read about financial topics typically found in college classes and in the news, as well as those related to your personal finances as a consumer and college student

Section 1

EXERCISE 1 Look at Word List 1.1 and the example sentences. Put a check mark in the box next to each word you already know. (POS stands for "part of speech.")

WORD LIST 1.1

Know it?	Word	POS	Example
☐	acquisition	*n.*	One way in which a corporation grows is through the **acquisition** of another, smaller company.
☐	approximate	*adj.*	The **approximate** cost of the car was $17,000.
		v.	He **approximated** his yearly income on the credit application.
☐	commission	*n.*	The **Comission** appointed by the governor made recommendations for the scholarship system.
		v.	She **commissioned** a report on diversity in the company.
☐	contribution	*n.*	He made a **contribution** to the aid organization.
☐	incentive	*n.*	The town offers tax **incentives** to companies that relocate there.
☐	investigation	*n.*	The government has begun an **investigation** into the business practices of Microsoft.
☐	minimum	*adj.*	You must maintain a **minimum** balance of $5.00.
		n.	She paid the **minimum** on her credit card balance.
☐	subsequent	*adj.*	The **subsequent** growth in the economy was a result of lowering the interest rate.

Master Student Tip   **Making Flash Cards**

To make flash cards, put the word on one side of an index card. On the other side, write any information you wish to remember about the word: definition, part of speech (POS), pronunciation, or perhaps a translation. Add more information to your card as you learn more about the word.

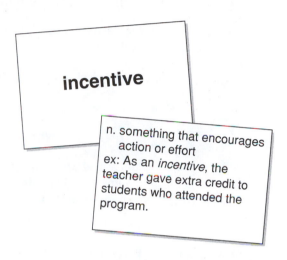

incentive

n. something that encourages action or effort
ex: As an *incentive*, the teacher gave extra credit to students who attended the program.

EXERCISE 2 Use a dictionary to check the meaning of all the words in Exercise 1. Then, make flash cards to study the words.

EXERCISE 3 Words often have multiple meanings. When using a dictionary, read all the entries, not just the first one. Examine the following meanings taken from the *American Heritage English as a Second Language Dictionary* entry for **commission**. Then write on each blank the number of the meaning that is being used. The first one has been done for you as an example.

com • mis • sion (*n.*)

Definitions

1. The act of granting authority to somebody to carry out a particular task or duty; the authority given by such a grant
2. A group of people who have been given authority by law to perform certain duties
3. The act of committing or doing something

4. Money in the form of a fee or percentage of a price paid to a salesperson or agent for services

5. Appointment to the rank of a commissioned officer in the armed forces

Sentences

1. ___2___ The Federal Trade **Commission** investigates false advertising.

2. _____ Captain Marcus received his **commission** in May 2002.

3. _____ Margo earns a **commission** on every item of clothing that she sells.

4. _____ The **commission** of fraud is a serious crime.

Master Student Tip **Antonyms and Synonyms**

If you associate a new vocabulary word with a synonym (a word that means almost the same thing) or with an antonym (a word that means the opposite) you may find it easier to remember the new word.

EXERCISE 4 Using a dictionary, match each of the bold vocabulary words with its antonym, or opposite. Write the correct letters on the lines.

1. _____ **minimum**
2. _____ **approximate**
3. _____ **acquisition**
4. _____ **subsequent**
5. _____ **incentive**

a. penalty
b. maximum
c. earlier
d. item sold
e. precise
f. after
g. amount

Master Student Tip **Suffixes**

A **suffix** is added to the end of a word or word stem. Learning to recognize common suffixes can help you identify the part of speech of a word and may help you relate the word to its word family. The -*tion* in *education* indicates that the word is a noun. *Education* and *educate* are members of the same word family. When you know common suffixes and word stems, it is easier to guess the meanings of new words that you meet.

EXERCISE 5 Two common suffixes that indicate a noun are *-tion* and *-sion*. These suffixes are usually added to verbs to form related nouns. These words are part of the same **word family.** *Commission* is an example of a noun that ends in *-sion*. It comes from the verb *commit*. Notice that the *t* in *commit* becomes an *s* before adding the suffix. Using a dictionary, complete the word family chart with the appropriate forms. Then use a member of the word family to complete the sentences below. Make the nouns singular or plural, and change the verb endings as necessary.

Verb	Noun
	acquisition
approximate	
	contribution
	investigation

1. The CEO of the company is under _____ for the misuse of company funds.

2. The price she told us for a semester of college was an _____; it varies with the number of credit hours you take.

3. We each made a _____ to the 9/11 relief fund.

4. Hossein's father is a lawyer who works in mergers and _____.

5. In addition to your company retirement plan, you should _____ regularly to an Individual Retirement Account (IRA).

6. People who invest their money in art often _____ a new piece at an auction.

Master Student Tip   **Using Flash Cards**

Use your flash cards to test yourself frequently over the words you are trying to learn. To learn a word, you must work with it many times, both in the exercises included in this book and on your own. One strategy is to go through your flashcards quickly as part of your routine to get ready for the day, and then again before you go to bed. You might carry them with you and flip through them quickly between classes. Find a time that works for you, and make it a habit to quiz yourself. Once you know a word, move it to a different stack that you review less frequently.

EXERCISE 6 Complete each of the following sentences with a vocabulary word from Word List 1.1. You may have to change the form of the word slightly. For example: *approximate, approximates, approximated,* or *approximation.* The first one has been done for you as an example.

1. The Alumni Association of the university asks graduates to make a ____contribution____ to the scholarship fund.

2. Sue works at Old Navy; she earns a _____ on all the clothing that she sells.

3. As an _____ to register early, the Study Abroad office offered $100 off the trip price to students who applied before December 1.

4. You must make a _____ deposit of $10 to open a savings account.

5. A special prosecutor has been assigned by the government to lead the _____ into the accounting practices of XYZ corporation.

6. The _____ of Computer General by XYZ corporation resulted in the closing of several stores.

7. Although after the initial interview Juanita was excited about working for the bank, the _____ interviews at corporate headquarters changed her mind.

Section 2

EXERCISE 7 Look at Word List 1.2 and the example sentences. Put a check mark in the box next to each word you already know.

WORD LIST 1.2

Know it?	Word	POS	Example
☐	consumer	*n.*	**Consumers** spent more money on travel this summer than in the two previous years.
☐	cycle	*n.*	The stock market moves in **cycles**.
☐	fee	*n.*	In addition to tuition, you must pay student **fees**.
☐	maintenance	*n.*	The **maintenance** of a good credit rating is important.
☐	obtain(ed)	*n.*	We **obtained** a loan.
☐	revenue	*n.*	You must report all your **revenue** on your tax forms.
☐	schedule	*n.*	The bank will give you a **schedule** for your loan payments.
		v.	We **scheduled** an appointment with the loan officer.
☐	sufficient	*adj.*	She did not have **sufficient** funds to go on the trip.

EXERCISE 8 Use a dictionary to check the meaning of the words in Word List 1.2. Then make flash cards to study the words.

Master Student Tip **Stress Patterns**

Stress patterns are one type of information you might include on your flash cards.

Pronunciation is part of knowing a word. Dictionaries use symbols to show you how to pronounce a word. They also separate the word into syllables and show you which syllable is stressed, or pronounced with more emphasis. Because syllable stress is more important than the pronunciation of individual sounds in English, we will use the following method for learning the pronunciation of new words.

Example word: *commission*   Dictionary: (kə-mĭsh´ən)

1. How many syllables does the word have? **3**
2. Which syllable is stressed the most? the 2nd
3. So it's a **3–2** word.

EXERCISE **9** Use a dictionary to classify the vocabulary words from Word List 1.2 by their stress pattern. The first one has been done for you.

1-1	2-1	2-2	3-1	3-2
				consumer

EXERCISE 10 Which word or words in each series below is *not* a synonym for the bold word? Put an X through the word or words that are not synonyms for the bold word.

1. **consumer**	buyer	eater	seller
2. **obtain**	acquire	get	lose
3. **cycle**	event	pattern	moment
4. **revenue**	expense	income	taxes
5. **fee**	price	discount	commission
6. **sufficient**	extra	adequate	enough
7. **maintenance**	deterioration	loss	preservation
8. **schedule**	timetable	information	program

EXERCISE 11 Work with a partner to answer the following questions. Think of synonyms for the words in bold. Compare your answers with those of other groups in the class.

1. What influences you to buy something as a **consumer**?

   _____

2. What are some typical sources of **revenue**?

   _____

3. A **schedule** of payments, such as the payments for a credit card, is usually set up on what type of **cycle**?

   _____

4. In what situations might you be required to pay a **fee**?

   _____

5. What suggestions could you give your state representative if the state government does not have **sufficient revenue** to cover the budget?

   _____

6. It is important to **maintain** a good credit rating.[1] How can you do that?

   _____

1. An indication of the risk involved in granting credit to people based on their history of paying bills and the amount of debt they have in relation to their income.

Section 3

EXERCISE 12 Look at Word List 1.3 and the example sentences. Put a check mark in the box next to each word you already know.

WORD LIST 1.3			
Know it?	**Word**	**POS**	**Example**
☐	**consistent**	*adj.*	Ronald Reagan, president of the United States in the 1980s, was a **consistent** supporter of the free-market economy.
☐	**export**	*n.*	Mexico's **exports** include oil, coffee, silver, and cotton.
		v.	Japan **exports** a lot of cars to the United States.
☐	**file**	*n.*	Keep a **file** of all your business expenses.
		v.	**File** your application before the deadline.
☐	**financial**	*adj.*	Remember to complete your **financial** aid application.
☐	**period**	*n.*	The 1990s were a **period** of rapid economic growth.
☐	**reliance**	*n.*	The U.S. **reliance** on foreign oil contributed to the oil crisis of the 1970s.
☐	**transfer**	*n.*	The **transfer** of stock from one person to another generally occurs by selling it, but stock may also be given as a gift.
		v.	I **transfer** money from my savings to my checking account.

EXERCISE 13 Use a dictionary to check the meanings of the words in Word List 1.3. Then make flash cards to study the words.

EXERCISE 14 The Students in Free Enterprise (SIFE) club is sponsoring a seminar called "Fiscal Fitness for Students." It is offering tips on staying in good shape **financially**. Help the club complete the tips by filling in the missing words.

a. period	**1.** Keep accurate _____ records. This will make it easier to _____ your taxes.
b. reliance	**2.** _____ on credit cards can be dangerous. Remember that you will have to pay for the purchases at the end of the month.
c. financial	**3.** If you pay for your credit card purchases during the grace _____ , you will not be charged interest.
d. file	**4.** _____ your savings to a separate account so that you will not be tempted to spend the money.
e. consistent	**5.** If you are trying to save money, put aside the same amount each month just as if you were paying a bill. It is important to be _____ and not skip a month.
f. transfer	

Can you think of other **financial** tips to give students?

_____

_____

_____

_____

EXERCISE 15 A common suffix used to create an adjective is the suffix *-al*. Sometimes a spelling change is made to the base form before the suffix is added. Complete the following chart with the correct adjective forms. Use a dictionary to check your spelling. Then use a word from the chart to complete each sentence below. The first sentence has been completed for you as an example.

Noun	Verb	Adjective
finance	finance	financial
promotion	promote	
period	—	
minimum	—	
cycle	cycle	

1. The company is in ____financial____ difficulty and may have to declare bankruptcy.

2. Consumer spending follows a _____ pattern, with spending increasing each year in the months prior to Christmas.

3. I received a _____ flyer in the mail for the new restaurant.

4. Scholarship recipients are subject to _____ review to ensure their continued eligibility for funds.

5. The goal of the new company was to develop an effective advertising campaign with _____ expenditure.

6. A mortgage is a type of loan used to _____ the purchase of a house.

7. Jose received a _____ at work; he is the new shift supervisor.

> **Master Student Tip** **Prefixes**
>
> Prefixes are added to the front of a word or word stem to change the meaning. An example of a common prefix is *dis-* as in *disapprove*. The majority of prefixes in English come from Latin or Greek. If your first language is a Romance language, such as Spanish or French, you will recognize many of them.

EXERCISE 16 The vocabulary words **export**, **subsequent**, and **transfer** each include a common prefix. Consider the meaning of these prefixes:

ex-   1. Former.   2. Outside, out of, away from.
sub-   1. Under, beneath.   2. A lower or secondary part.
trans- 1. Across, beyond.   2. Change.

With a partner, think of as many words as you can that begin with these prefixes. Then find some additional words in a dictionary. Write them on the lines below. Did you find any that you knew already, but forgot?

ex-	*sub-*	*trans-*
_____	_____	_____
_____	_____	_____
_____	_____	_____

Section 4

CHAPTER 1 REVIEW

EXERCISE 17 Before continuing with the review exercises, use your flash cards to test yourself on the words from the chapter. Do you know the part of speech? Can you write a sentence using the word?

acquisition	cycle	investigation	revenue
approximate	export	maintenance	schedule
commission	fee	minimum	subsequent
consistent	file	obtain	sufficient
consumer	financial	period	transfer
contribution	incentive	reliance	

EXERCISE 18 Analyze the stress patterns of all the words in the chapter, using the method you learned in Exercise 9.

1-1	
2-1	export
2-2	export
3-1	
3-2	
4-1	
4-2	
4-3	
5-4	

EXERCISE 19 College students get many mail offers for credit cards. Complete the following letter from a credit card company. Use the appropriate vocabulary word from the word bank. Use each word only once.

fee	incentive	minimum	cycle	period

Dear Student,

When you are in college, you have many needs: textbooks, supplies, a computer . . . . Our Gold card will allow you to make these purchases now and spread the payments out over a _____ of time. Get what you need, when you need it. Each month you will receive a statement of your account. When you receive your statement, you may pay the entire bill, or you may make payments over the next several months. You must make the _____ payment listed on the statement. There is no annual membership _____. As a further _____ to accept our offer, you will earn a 5% rebate on all your purchases for the first billing _____. Simply complete the enclosed application and return it. Hurry, this offer ends September 1st!

Sincerely,

John Smith

Director of New Accounts

WEB POWER

You will find additional exercises related to the content in this chapter at **elt.heinle.com/collegevocab**.

Founding Principles

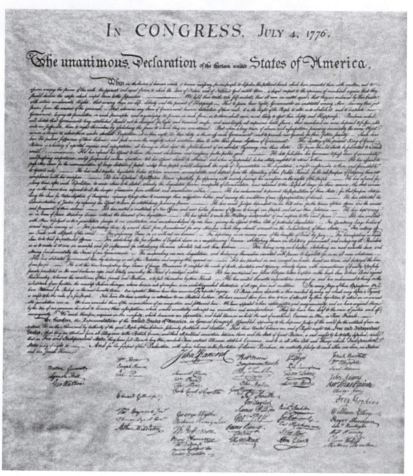

In this chapter, you will

▶ **Become familiar with twenty-four academic vocabulary words**

▶ **Practice recognizing common suffixes**

▶ **Increase your knowledge of word families**

▶ **Learn about collocations**

▶ **Read about political science and the government of the United States**

Section 1

EXERCISE **1** Look at Word List 2.1 and the example sentences. Put a check mark in the box next to each word you already know. (POS stands for "part of speech.")

WORD LIST 2.1

Know it?	Word	POS	Example
☐	author	n.	James Madison was one of the **authors** of the *Federalist Papers*.
☐	commitment	n.	They stated their **commitment** to a democracy.
☐	consent	v.	George Washington **consented** to be the first president.
		n.	A legitimate government is based on the people's **consent**.
☐	derive	v.	The Founding Fathers' ideas of government **derive** from eighteenth-century political philosophy.
☐	notion	n.	The most important **notion** was the idea of a limited government.
☐	philosophy	n.	The Founding Fathers' ideas of government derive from eighteenth-century political **philosophy**.
☐	pursue	v.	They **pursued** their goal of independence.
☐	vision	n.	They had a **vision** for the future of their country.

EXERCISE 2 Read and discuss the following paragraph about the Declaration of Independence. With a partner, figure out the meanings of the words in bold. Check your guesses by looking up the words in a dictionary. Then make flash cards to study the words.

THE DECLARATION OF INDEPENDENCE

The Founding Fathers[1] of the United States of America had a **vision** of the kind of government they wanted based on the **philosophy** of the Enlightenment and on the system of government they observed among the Native Americans. One of the primary principles of this **philosophy** was that all men are created equal. They also believed that true government **derives** its power from the **consent** of the people. In the Declaration of Independence, the Founding Fathers stated their **commitment** to a democratic form of government, their belief in the equality of all men, and the **notion** that man has a right to **pursue** happiness. The primary **author** of the Declaration of Independence was Thomas Jefferson.

1. The Founding Fathers were the political leaders in the American colonies who came together to declare independence from Great Britian and to establish a new form of goverment in the 1770s.

EXERCISE 3 Match each bold vocabulary word with the word or words that are closest in meaning. Write the correct letters on the lines.

1. __c__ author
2. _____ commitment
3. _____ consent
4. _____ derive
5. _____ notion
6. _____ philosophy
7. _____ pursue
8. _____ vision

a. to follow or strive for
b. a note
c. a writer
d. an idea
e. an image
f. to send
g. a belief system
h. to come from something
i. a dedication to something
j. to agree to something

Master Student Tip   **Collocations**

Collocations are words that commonly occur together. *Peanut butter* and *jelly* are collocations, but so are words like *register* and *for*, as in "I need to register for classes." When you learn new vocabulary, look for collocations.

EXERCISE 4 Match the sentence halves to form complete sentences. Then write the sentences on the lines below. Use collocations to help you match the sentence halves. The first one has been done for you as an example.

1. __g__ George Washington's **commitment**
2. _____ The **philosophy** of John Locke
3. _____ Benjamin Franklin was one
4. _____ Their **notion** of equality
5. _____ The just power of a government is **derived**
6. _____ The colonists **pursued**
7. _____ There were two opposing **visions** for the government:

a. of the **authors** of the Declaration of Independence.
b. from the **consent** of the governed.
c. influenced the Founding Fathers.
d. the goal of independence.
e. was limited to free white men.
f. a strong central government and a confederation similar to that of the Iroquois Indians.
g. to the republic was evident.

1. <u>George Washington's commitment to the new republic was evident.</u>

2. _____

3. _____

4. _____

5. _____

6. _____

7. _____

EXERCISE 5 Look at the way the following vocabulary words have been used in the other exercises and in the examples in your dictionary. Fill in the chart below with the collocations you have noticed for these vocabulary words. Pay particular attention to prepositions.

author	of
commitment	
consent	
derive	
notion	

Master Student Tip **Vocabulary Journal**

A **vocabulary journal** can be a useful tool for learning new vocabulary. All you need is a blank notebook. In it you can write down the new words you encounter when you are reading, their definitions, and other important information about the words. You might divide your notebook into sections, with a different section for each course you are taking. This is a good way to learn new words that are specific to one academic discipline. An example is the word *neurosis* in the discipline of psychology.

Section 2

EXERCISE 6 Look at Word List 2.2 and the example sentences. Put a check mark in the box next to each word you already know.

WORD LIST 2.2			
Know it?	**Word**	**POS**	**Example**
☐	abstract	*adj.*	Happiness is an **abstract** concept.
		n.	I found an **abstract** of the article my professor suggested on the Constitution.
☐	draft	*n.*	There were several **drafts** of the Constitution before the final version was agreed upon.
		v.	Jefferson **drafted** the Declaration of Independence, and then the others suggested changes.
☐	federal	*adj.*	I pay **federal** and state taxes.
☐	framework	*n.*	James Madison shaped the **framework** of our national government.
☐	implementation	*n.*	Congress makes the laws, but the executive branch is responsible for their **implementation**.
☐	media	*n.*	A free press and other **media** are essential to democracy.
☐	quotation	*n.*	Many phrases in the Declaration of Independence resemble **quotations** from John Locke.
☐	specify	*v.*	The Constitution **specifies** the responsibilities of each branch of government.

EXERCISE [7] Read and discuss the following paragraph about the Constitution. With a partner, figure out the meanings of the bold words. Check your guesses by looking up the words in a dictionary. Then make flash cards to study the words.

THE CONSTITUTION

"We the People of the United States, in Order to form a more perfect Union, . . ." This famous **quotation** is the beginning of the Constitution. The Declaration of Independence did not **specify** anything about the **implementation** of a democratic form of government. In establishing the structure of the government, the Founding Fathers were influenced by the system of confederation they observed among the Native American Indian tribes. It is the Constitution that gives us the **framework** for our **federal** government. The original **draft** did not include the Bill of Rights, which is the most familiar part of the document. It is here that we find the First Amendment, which, among other things, protects the right of the **media** to write and speak the news freely. The Bill of Rights guarantees those individual rights that make up the more **abstract** idea of freedom. Among other things, these rights include freedom of speech, freedom of religion, the right to assemble peacefully, the right to petition the government, and the right to bear arms.

Master Student Tip   Word Families

A **word family** is a group of words that are related in meaning but that have different grammatical forms. For example, *specify* is a verb, and *specific* is an adjective, but both words have to do with being precise. Learning to recognize different words as part of the same word family can help you expand your vocabulary.

EXERCISE 8   Use a dictionary and the knowledge you have of suffixes to complete the word family chart. Sometimes the same word can be two parts of speech.

Verb	Noun	Adjective
	draft	
	implementation	
abstract	abstraction	abstract
specify		
		federal
	quotation	

Which part of speech is indicated by the following suffixes?

-tion _____noun_____

-al _____

-ic _____

EXERCISE 9   Match each of the vocabulary words with its antonym, or opposite. Write the correct letters on the lines.

1. _____ abstract

2. _____ draft

3. _____ federal

4. _____ generalize

a. specify
b. local
c. concrete
d. final version

EXERCISE 10 Complete each sentence with a vocabulary word from Word List 2.2.

1. The president began his speech with a ___*quotation*___ from the Declaration of Independence.

2. In his State of the Union address, the president announced that he would _____ new legislation on education to send to Congress.

3. The president did not _____ how he would reach his education goals.

4. He recognized that education is primarily the responsibility of the state government, not the _____ government.

5. However, <u>financial</u> incentives will be linked to the _____ of his goals.

6. The _____ criticized the president.

7. The journalists said that his goals were too _____, but perhaps the draft of the new law will provide a _____ to guide the states in trying to reach the president's goals.

EXERCISE 11 Discuss the following questions with a partner. Write your answers on the lines provided.

1. Think of a famous person whose words are important to you. Can you remember a **quotation** from what that person said or wrote? What is it? Who said it?

_____

_____

2. When the Constitution was written, the only form of **media** that existed was the written press. What forms of **media** do we have today?

_____

_____

3. The United States has **federal**, state, and local governments. What do you think the differences are between these three forms of government?

   _____

   _____

4. What sort of things can you **implement**?

   _____

   _____

5. When you write a paper, how do you begin your first **draft**?

   _____

   _____

6. Can you think of a synonym for **framework**? What is it?

   _____

   _____

Master Student Tip | **Word Pictures**

One way of learning new vocabulary is to create a word picture that helps you remember the meaning. For example, to learn the word *framework* you might think of the frame of a house. The frame is like the skeleton of a house; it provides the structure for the house. So, a **framework** provides a structure for something. Can you make word pictures for any of the other words you have studied so far?

Section 3

EXERCISE **12** Look at Word List 2.3 and the example sentences. Put a check mark in the box next to each word you already know.

WORD LIST 2.3

Know it?	Word	POS	Example
☐	concentration	*n.*	Although there is a **concentration** of political power in Washington, D.C., it is not the center of economic power for the United States.
☐	emphasis	*n.*	In James Madison's framework for the government, the **emphasis** is on the separation and balance of powers.
☐	ensure	*v.*	The Constitution was written in part to **ensure** "the Blessings of Liberty" for future generations.
☐	grant	*v.*	The Constitution **granted** specific powers to the federal government and to the state governments.
☐	legislation	*n.*	**Legislation** originates in Congress, but the president must sign a bill for it to become law.
☐	mechanism	*n.*	The American government is a very complex **mechanism**.
☐	military	*n.*	The **military** is under the control of the president.
☐	participation	*n.*	The direct **participation** of the people is limited in the American democracy.

EXERCISE 13 Read and discuss the paragraph on page 28 about the Constitution. With a partner, figure out the meaning of the bold words. Check your guesses by looking up the words in a dictionary. Then make flash cards to study the words.

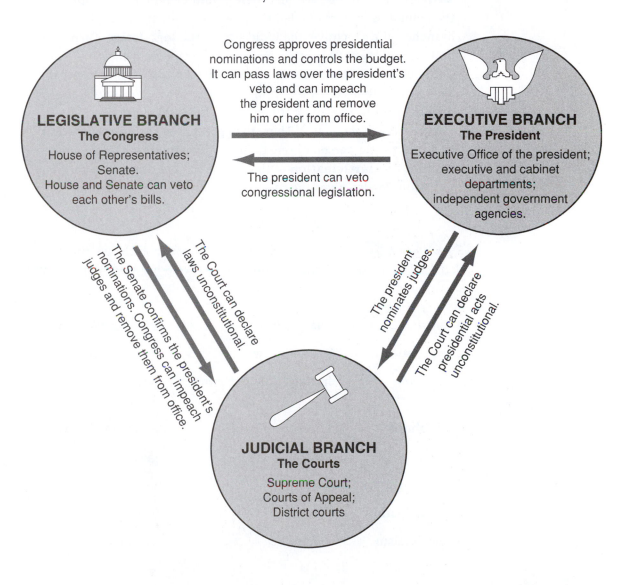

Congress approves presidential nominations and controls the budget. It can pass laws over the president's veto and can impeach the president and remove him or her from office.

LEGISLATIVE BRANCH
The Congress

House of Representatives; Senate.
House and Senate can veto each other's bills.

The president can veto congressional legislation.

EXECUTIVE BRANCH
The President

Executive Office of the president; executive and cabinet departments; independent government agencies.

The Senate confirms the president's nominations. Congress can impeach judges and remove them from office.

The Court can declare laws unconstitutional.

The president nominates judges.

The Court can declare presidential acts unconstitutional.

JUDICIAL BRANCH
The Courts

Supreme Court;
Courts of Appeal;
District courts

THE CONSTITUTION

In the Constitution, the **emphasis** is on the structure of the government. To **ensure** that there would be no king or emperor, the Founding Fathers divided the power to govern among three branches: the executive, the judicial, and the **legislative**. Each branch was **granted** specific powers. The framers of the Constitution created a **mechanism** of checks and balances so that each branch limited the power of the other two. For example, the president is Commander-in-Chief of the **military**; but only Congress can declare war. Thus, they prevented the **concentration** of power in one person or one branch of government. A democracy requires the **participation** of the people in government, so the Constitution also gives the rules for electing Congress and the president.

EXERCISE 14 Underline the word or phrase in each row that is related to the bold vocabulary word. The first one has been done for you as an example.

1. **ensure**	<u>guarantee</u>	buy insurance for
2. **legislation**	making a law	judging a court case
3. **military**	having to do with a mill	having to do with the armed forces
4. **emphasis**	importance	based on observation
5. **grant**	grab	give
6. **concentration**	circle	focus on something
7. **participation**	join in	leave
8. **mechanism**	a machine	a desire

EXERCISE 15 Use a dictionary to complete the word family chart below. Compare your answers with a classmate's.

Noun	Person	Verb	Adjective	Adverb
military	militant	militarize	**military**	militarily
legislation				—
participation				—
mechanism				
emphasis	—			
grant			—	—

Part of knowing a word is recognizing which part of speech it is. Suffixes can help you do that. Which part of speech is indicated by the following suffixes?

-tion _____noun_____   -ant _____

-ate _____   -or _____

-ize _____   -ly _____

-ism _____   -ic _____

Master Student Tip   **Root Stem**

The word part that the suffix or prefix attaches to is the **root stem**. Many common root stems in English come from Latin or Greek. If you speak a Romance language, such as Spanish or French, you may recognize some of them already. Learning these root stems can help you guess the meanings of new words.

EXERCISE **16** These common root stems are useful to know. See how many additional words you can think of that have the same root stem. Write them in the chart. Compare your completed chart with another student's.

Stem	Example	Additional words
leg- from the Latin word for "law"	legislation	
vis- meaning "see"	vision	
port- meaning "carry"	export	

EXERCISE 17 Match the first half of the sentence with the part that logically completes it. Then write the sentences on the lines below. The first one has been done for you as an example.

1. __g__ The Constitution **grants**

2. _____ The role of the **military**

3. _____ New **legislation**

4. _____ The **emphasis** in the Bill of Rights

5. _____ The Supreme Court **ensures**

6. _____ There is a **mechanism** by which

7. _____ What can we do to encourage

8. _____ The United States has not achieved economic equality;

a. the constitutionality of new laws.

b. is on the rights of the individual.

c. wealth is **concentrated** in the hands of a few.

d. Congress may override the president's veto.

e. is to protect and defend the country.

f. is enacted by the Congress.

g. certain powers to the Supreme Court.

h. broader **participation** in the election?

1. The Constitution grants certain powers to the Supreme Court.

2. _____

3. _____

4. _____

5. _____

6. _____

7. _____

8. _____

Section 4

EXERCISE **18** Before continuing with the review exercises, use your flash cards to test yourself on the words from the chapter.

abstract	draft	implementation	participation
author	emphasis	legislation	philosophy
commitment	ensure	mechanism	pursue
concentration	federal	media	quotation
consent	framework	military	specify
derive	grant	notion	vision

EXERCISE **19** Group all the words in the chapter by their pronunciation pattern using the method you learned in Chapter 1. One has been done for you as an example.

1-1	
2-1	
2-2	
3-1	
3-2	
4-1	
4-2	
4-3	*concentration*
5-4	

EXERCISE 20 In each of the following groups, match the definition on the left to a word on the right. You will not use all the words. The first one has been done for you as an example.

A.

1. ___c___ A basic theory; a viewpoint

2. _____ A person who writes

3. _____ To state clearly or in detail

4. _____ Special forcefulness of expression that gives importance

5. _____ A rough outline or plan

a. draft
b. abstract
c. philosophy
d. emphasis
e. specify
f. author
g. ensure
h. derive

B.

1. _____ Journalists as a group

2. _____ A mental picture

3. _____ To try to gain or accomplish

4. _____ A promise or obligation

5. _____ To repeat words written or said

a. commitment
b. notion
c. quote
d. framework
e. consent
f. pursue
g. media
h. vision

C.

1. _____ To give or allow

2. _____ Involvement in something

3. _____ Relating to the armed forces

4. _____ A system of parts that work together

5. _____ The act of giving close, undivided attention

a. concentration
b. implementation
c. federal
d. grant
e. legislation
f. military
g. mechanism
h. participation

WEB POWER

You will find additional exercises related to the content in this chapter at **elt.heinle.com/collegevocab**.

Math Problems

In this chapter, you will

- ► Become familiar with twenty-four new words from the Academic Word List
- ► Distinguish between the **literal** and **figurative** meanings of words
- ► Learn new **suffixes**
- ► Become familiar with vocabulary used to discuss mathematics and related issues

Section 1

EXERCISE 1 Look at Word List 3.1. Put a check mark in the box next to each word you know already. (The chart heading POS stands for "part of speech.")

Know it?	Word	POS	Example
☐	**area**	*n.*	The **area** of a rectangle is equal to the height times the width.
☐	**dimension**	*n.*	A square has two **dimensions**; a cube has three.
☐	**equation**	*n.*	"2 + 4 = 6" is an example of an **equation**.
☐	**negative**	*adj.*	**Negative** numbers have values less than zero.
☐	**plus**	*conj.*	Two **plus** four equals six.
☐	**prime**	*adj.*	Seven is a **prime** number.
☐	**ratio**	*n.*	Pi (π) is used to express the **ratio** of the radius to the circumference of a circle.
☐	**volume**	*n.*	A sphere has **volume**; a circle does not.

WORD LIST 3.1

EXERCISE 2 Use a dictionary to find the definitions of the words in Word List 3.1. Then make flash cards to study the words.

Master Student Tip   **Literal and Figurative Meanings**

Words can often be used **literally** or **figuratively**. The **literal** meaning is the most basic or concrete meaning of the word. The **figurative** meaning is a more abstract or imaginative meaning. For example, the word *plus* can be used to indicate addition in a math *equation*. This is the literal meaning. However, if we say that something *is a plus*, we mean that it is an added or unexpected benefit. This second use of the word *plus* is a figurative meaning.

EXERCISE 3   Examine the sentences below. Write L if you think the vocabulary word is being used in a literal way. Write F if you think it is being used in a figurative way. Then see if you can think of other examples to share with the class.

1. ___L___ The **dimensions** of the house are specified in the blueprints prepared by the architect.

2. _____ Martine had a **negative** reaction to the medicine the doctor prescribed.

3. _____ The **prime** candidate for the position was a woman from Missouri.

4. _____ There is a political **dimension** to the healthcare debate.

5. _____ The Pythagorean theorem is summarized by the **equation** $a^2 + b^2 = c^2$.

6. _____ Her **area** of expertise is molecular biology.

7. _____ A **prime** number cannot be divided evenly by any other number but itself and one.

8. _____ The restaurant bill included the cost of dinner **plus** 15 percent for service because we were a large group.

9. _____ The fish tank had a **volume** of two gallons.

10. _____ Speaking several languages is a real **plus** when applying for a job.

11. _____ The temperature in New Hampshire was **negative** 10 yesterday.

12. _____ The volleyball court is located in the **area** east of the Student Center.

13. _____ Due to the heavy **volume** of traffic near the school, the city decided to widen the road.

14. _____ Regular exercise is part of the **equation** for good health.

EXERCISE 4 Rearrange the jumbled words to make a sentence. As you try to unscramble the sentences, think about the placement of adjectives in relationship to nouns and any collocations you noticed with the words in Word List 3.1.

1. was / The patient's / **negative** / test / the flu / for

   The patient's test for the flu was negative.

2. **area** / There / in / the / are / houses / many / new

   _____

3. are / the table / the **dimensions** / What / of / ?

   _____

4. books / pays for / The scholarship / tuition / **plus**

   _____

5. What / the **ratio** / of / is / boys / in / the class / to / girls / ?

   _____

6. the **equation** / to solve / The student / unable / in algebra / was

   _____

7. concern / The safety / was / of / the children / **prime** / her

   _____

8. **volume** / equal / A liter / not / a gallon / do /and / have

   _____

EXERCISE 5 With a partner, answer the following questions. You will need a measuring tape or yardstick for the first one.

1. What are the **dimensions** of your table or desk? Are all the desks in the class the same size?
2. Now, calculate the **area** of the table or desktop. (*Hint*: Multiply height times width.)
3. What is the **ratio** of men to women in your class? Is this typical of your other classes?
4. How many **prime** numbers are between 0 and 20?
5. Do you have **negative** temperatures in the winter where you live now? In the place you are from?
6. Name some restaurants in the **area**. Which ones would you recommend to a friend?
7. In the **equation** for success in school, what do you consider to be the **prime** factors?
8. At what hour of the day is the **volume** of traffic on the roads the heaviest?
9. "3-D" is an abbreviated way of saying "three **dimensions**." How can a movie be 3-D?

> **Master Student Tip**   **Pronunciation**
>
> The suffixes *-sion* and *-tion* both indicate a noun, and both are pronounced *shən*.

EXERCISE 6 With a partner, see how many words you can think of that end with the same sound as *equation* and *dimension*. Group the words according to their endings and write the words in the chart.

-tion	*-sion*

Section 2

EXERCISE 7 Look at Word List 3.2. Put a check mark in the box next to each word you know already.

WORD LIST 3.2			
Know it?	**Word**	**POS**	**Example**
☐	**gender**	*n.*	One's ability in math is not related to **gender**.
☐	**intelligence**	*n.*	Logical-mathematical **intelligence** is one of eight types of **intelligence** proposed by Howard Gardner.
☐	**apparent**	*adj.*	There are **apparent** differences in the math ability of girls and boys.
☐	**capable**	*adj.*	Girls are **capable** of doing well in math when they are motivated.
☐	**expert**	*n.*	**Experts** do not agree on the causes of these differences.
☐	**logic**	*n.*	Students who are "math smart" often use **logic** and are problem solvers.
☐	**promote**	*v.*	Many programs **promote** success in math among girls.
☐	**equivalent**	*adj.*	Research indicates that girls and boys do not have **equivalent** experiences in school.

EXERCISE 8 Read the following paragraph about the connection between gender and math ability. Discuss the bold vocabulary with a partner. Guess the meanings of the new words. Check your guesses in a dictionary, and then make flash cards to study the words.

ARE YOU MATH SMART?

"Boys are better in math than girls." "Girls just can't do math." Statements like these are common, but are they true? Do boys have better skills in **logic** than girls?

Experts do not agree on the explanation for the **apparent** differences in the girls' and boys' performance in math. However, some studies show that girls are just as **capable** of doing math as boys. These studies suggest that differences in performance are not due to **gender**, to biological differences in **intelligence**, but rather, seem to be influenced by the learning environment. Boys and girls typically do not have **equivalent** experiences in math class. Boys tend to receive more of the teacher's time and attention. Boys are encouraged to study math more than girls. Thanks to programs that **promote** the study of math among girls, the gap in their performance is diminishing.

Source: Campbell, P. (1991, June). "Girls and math: Enough is known for action." *WEEA Digest.* Retrieved from www.edc.org/WomensEquity/pubs/digests/digest-math.html

Master Student Tip   **Synonyms**

Remember that **synonyms** are words that have the same, or nearly the same, meaning. When you make your flash cards, you may want to write down a synonym for the new vocabulary word in addition to the definition.

EXERCISE 9 Match each bold vocabulary word with its synonym. The first one has been done for you as an example. You will not use all the synonyms.

1. ___c___ gender

2. _____ intelligence

3. _____ apparent

4. _____ capable

5. _____ expert

6. _____ logic

7. _____ promote

8. _____ equivalent

a. reason
b. the same
c. sex
d. able
e. a professional
f. competitive
g. the ability to understand
h. clear
i. encourage
j. promise

Master Student Tip

When studying vocabulary, it is important to regularly go back and review the words you have studied in previous chapters. This **repetition** is essential for learning a word. It is equally important that the repetitions be *spaced out over time*, but not so far apart that you completely forget the word. At the end of every chapter, go back and review all the words you have learned so far.

EXERCISE 10 Howard Gardner has proposed a theory of multiple **intelligences** that suggests 8 different types of **intelligence**.

They are: linguistic intelligence, logical-mathematical intelligence, spatial intelligence, bodily-kinesthetic intelligence, musical intelligence, interpersonal intelligence, intrapersonal intelligence, and naturalist intelligence. Use the internet to research the theory of multiple intelligences, then write a paragraph describing the way in which you are smart.

EXERCISE 11 Fill in each blank with a vocabulary word from Word List 3.2. You may have to change the form of the word slightly. For instance, you may need to make it plural rather than singular. The first one has been done for you as an example.

1. While there is no ___*apparent*___ difference in math ability among boys and girls, there is a difference in the level of interest in math between the _____. This lack of interest influences girls' performance.

2. _____ say that if we do not _____ an interest in math among young women, we will continue to have few women in career fields such as computers and engineering.

3. In math, boys may seem to excel more than girls, but in language skills, girls appear to be more _____.

4. Gardner's research shows many different ways of looking at _____: logical-mathematical, visual-spatial, bodily-kinesthetic, verbal-linguistic, naturalist, musical-rhythmic, interpersonal, and intrapersonal **intelligence.**

5. The two types of _____ are inductive and deductive.

6. Some researchers advocate teaching boys and girls in separate but _____ programs for math and science.

Master Student Tip   **Suffixes**

Remember that suffixes can indicate a word's part of speech. Sometimes a suffix can indicate more than one part of speech. To become more aware of suffixes, keep a list of suffixes you encounter and the part or parts of speech they indicate. Keep this list on one of your flash cards or in a vocabulary journal.

EXERCISE 12 Complete this word family chart. The first row has been done for you as an example. Use a dictionary to check the different forms of each word. Then answer the questions below.

Verb	Noun-person	Noun	Adjective	Adverb
promote	promoter	promotion	promotional	—
—	—	—	apparent	
—	—		capable	
—	expert			
—		logic		
—		intelligence		

1. Which word can be two different parts of speech? _____

   What are those two parts of speech? _____

2. Which suffix indicates an adverb? _____

3. Which suffixes indicate an adjective? _____

4. Which suffixes indicate a noun? _____

EXERCISE 13 Complete each sentence with a word from the word family chart in Exercise 12.

1. A *think tank* is a group of advisers composed of _____ and experts in a specific field.

2. We received some coupons and other _____ material for the new restaurant in the mail.

3. _____, his reaction does not make sense; he responded emotionally to the situation.

4. Soo is a very _____ person; she will do the job well.

5. Juan's _____ in immigration law is well known.

6. The detective said that the _____ cause of death was a heart attack; there does not seem to have been foul play.

Section 3

EXERCISE 14 Look at Word List 3.3. Put a check mark in the box next to each word you know already.

WORD LIST 3.3

Know it?	Word	POS	Example
☐	category	*n.*	A square, a rectangle, and a rhombus all belong to the geometric **category** of parallelograms.
☐	display	*v.*	The math club **displayed** the problems for the contest and their solutions on the bulletin board.
		n.	A **display** in the math building honors great mathematicians.
☐	distinct	*adj.*	An isosceles triangle is **distinct** from other triangles in that two of its sides are of equal length.
☐	feature	*n.*	A square combines the key **features** of a rectangle with those of a rhombus.
☐	highlight	*v.*	Although the division of the curriculum into algebra, geometry, and trigonometry **highlights** the differences, all math is related.
☐	input	*n.*	A computer simulation is only as good as its **input**.
☐	instructions	*n.*	Always read the **instructions** carefully before beginning a problem.
☐	parameter	*n.*	The word *parameter* has a different meaning in different fields, but its origin is in mathematics.

EXERCISE 15 Use a dictionary to check definitions, and then make flash cards for the words in Word List 3.3.

EXERCISE 16 For each row, circle the word or words that are synonyms for the bold vocabulary word.

1. **category**	(group)	(classification)	catalog
2. **display**	show	dissimulate	hide
3. **distinct**	dead	separate	clear
4. **feature**	characteristic	element	fact
5. **highlight**	lamp	color	emphasize
6. **input**	data	energy	information
7. **instructions**	problems	tests	guidelines
8. **parameters**	boundaries	limits	restrictions

Master Student Tip   **Word Stems**

The very common word stem -*meter* comes from the Greek, meaning "to measure." An example is the word *chronometer*. *Chrono*- is a word stem meaning "time." *Chronometer* is another word for *stopwatch*. Becoming familiar with these common word stems will help you learn new vocabulary.

EXERCISE 17 The word *parameter* has many different meanings that are specific to the context in which it is being used, whether that is astronomy or statistics or electricity. However, in all cases, the meaning is related to the idea of establishing limits or boundaries for what is possible. The word stem -*meter*- means "to measure." On the lines below, list as many words as you can think of that end in -*meter*. Then write the meanings. Are the meanings of those words related to measurement?

Word	**Meaning**
_____	_____
_____	_____
_____	_____
_____	_____

EXERCISE 18 Match the first half of the sentence with the part that logically completes it. The first one has been done for you as an example.

1. __d__ The distinguishing **feature** of a right triangle is

2. _____ Before beginning a test, one should

3. _____ The Oscars are divided into several **categories:**

4. _____ One of the **highlights** of the trip

5. _____ In honor of Black History Month the library has a **display**

6. _____ If you do not complete the practice problems, there is a **distinct** possibility

7. _____ Once you have established the equations that define each column in the Excel spreadsheet, all you have to do is

8. _____ All projects entered in the contest must

a. that you will fail the algebra test.

b. was our visit to the Louvre museum in Paris.

c. **input** the data, and the program will calculate the results.

d. that it has a ninety-degree angle.

e. **featuring** famous African-American writers such as Maya Angelou and Richard Wright.

f. stay within the **parameters** established for the competition.

g. Best Actor, Best Actress, Best screenplay, Best Song, etc.

h. read all the **instructions**.

EXERCISE 19 Complete the following activities, and discuss them with a partner.

1. Follow these **instructions** carefully.
   a. Draw each of the following geometric figures and label them.
      circle   square   triangle   sphere
      cone   rectangle   cube
   b. Create two or more **categories** based on a **distinct feature**, and then classify the figures according to those **categories**.

2. When you read a textbook, do you **highlight** parts of the text? Discuss which parts of the text you **highlight**. How much of the text should you **highlight**?

3. What sorts of things can be **displayed**? Where do you typically see a **display**?

4. In addition to computer science, in what other disciplines is the word *input* used? Give an example of **input**.

Section 4

CHAPTER 3 REVIEW

EXERCISE 20 Before continuing with the review exercises, use your flash cards to test yourself on the vocabulary words from the chapter.

apparent	distinct	highlight	parameter
area	equation	input	plus
capable	equivalent	instructions	prime
category	expert	intelligence	promote
dimension	feature	logic	ratio
display	gender	negative	volume

EXERCISE 21 Group all the words in the chapter by their pronunciation pattern. One has been completed for you as an example.

1-1	
2-1	
2-2	
3-1	
3-2	
4-1	*category*
4-2	

Notice the pronunciation patterns of words that can be both a noun and a verb. Is the pronunciation for the noun and the verb the same or different?

47

EXERCISE 22 Use words from the list in Exercise 20 to complete the puzzle.

Across

1. Separate or different

5. The measurement of length, width, or thickness

7. Added to

8. To mark the important parts of a text

11. A proportion

12. Clear reasoning

13. Most important

15. Mental ability

19. Of equal value

21. Seeming

22. Amount

23. A fixed limit or boundary

Down

2. Ideas, money, or work put into a project

3. Directions

4. A class or division in a system of classification

6. Not positive

9. To aid the progress of something

10. Able

14. Sexual identity

16. A mathematical statement that two expressions are equal

17. A prominent characteristic

18. To put something to be seen in public

19. A person with great knowledge or skill

20. Region

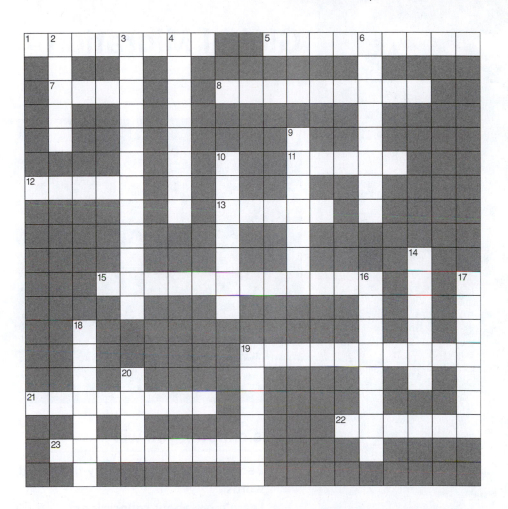

Global Migration

In this chapter, you will

▶ Become familiar with twenty-three academic vocabulary words

▶ Learn more about **collocations**

▶ Expand your knowledge of **word families**

▶ Read about sociology and the movement of people

Section 1

EXERCISE 1 Look at Word List 4.1 and the example sentences. Put a check mark in the box next to each word you already know. Leave the third column blank for now. (POS stands for "part of speech.")

Know it?	Word	POS	Example
☐	**estate**		Historically, the oldest son of a nobleman inherited the family **estate**.
☐	**global**		The movement of people from one area to another is a **global** phenomenon.
☐	**migration**		**Migration** is a constant part of human history.
☐	**motivation**		The **motivation** to leave home is often a combination of positive and negative factors.
☐	**overseas**		Some people move **overseas** permanently; for others it is a temporary move. Her **overseas** trip had been a lifelong dream.
☐	**principal**		What is the **principal** force behind human migration?
☐	**response**		Sometimes people leave their homes in **response** to natural disasters such as floods and famines.
☐	**survive**		Migration can be dangerous; sometimes people do not **survive** the trip.

WORD LIST 4.1

EXERCISE 2 Read and discuss with a partner the following passage about human migration. Can you and your partner figure out the meaning of the bold vocabulary words? Check your guesses by looking up the words in a dictionary. Then, make flash cards to study the words.

HUMAN MIGRATION

Human **migration** has occurred throughout history. In times of famine or other natural disaster, early humans moved to other areas in order to **survive**. The **response** of humans to disasters, whether natural or man-made, has frequently been the same. In the history of the United States, the promise of a better life drew many early colonists from Europe **overseas** to the New World. In Europe, it was difficult for those who had no family **estate** to obtain land. In the American colonies, settlers could have their own land, but they usually displaced the native peoples already living there.

Migration is not limited to one area of the world, but occurs today on a **global** scale. Patterns of **migration** change in **response** to different events. Economic **motivation** seems to be the **principal** influence on human **migration** now, but the reality is often a complex mix of factors. War, religion, government policies, political upheaval, and economic hardship all play a role in the movement of humans across the face of Earth.

EXERCISE 3 Study the example sentences in Word List 4.1 and in the paragraph above. Then use a dictionary to help you determine the part of speech of each bold word. Fill in the third column in Word List 4.1. Be sure to note the part of speech on your flash cards.

EXERCISE 4 Match the bold vocabulary word with the correct definition.

1. _____ **principal**
2. _____ **motivation**
3. _____ **overseas**
4. _____ **estate**
5. _____ **global**
6. _____ **survive**
7. _____ **response**
8. _____ **migration**

a. a large piece of land
b. movement from one country to another
c. to stay alive
d. first in importance
e. the act of responding
f. abroad
g. worldwide
h. the reason for doing something
i. motorized movement
j. on the ocean

Master Student Tip   **Collocations**

Collocations are patterns of words that frequently appear together, such as *make a reservation*. A collocation also refers to word combinations such as *global warming*, *global economy*, and *global tracking system*, but *global person* is not a collocation because these two words do not often appear together. When you learn new vocabulary, look for collocations and include them on your flash cards or in your vocabulary journal.

EXERCISE 5 In the following sentences, cross out the choice in parentheses that is not appropriate. Use a dictionary and the examples in the text above to check collocations.

1. The Donner party was a group of settlers who headed west to California from Illinois before the great western **migration** (of, for) settlers began on the Oregon trail.
2. The disaster that befell the group was not due to (lack of, less) **motivation.**
3. Stranded in the Rocky Mountains in the winter of 1846, the Donner party ate human flesh (in order to, for) **survive**.
4. Although in most cultures it is forbidden to eat humans, cannibalism sometimes occurs in **response** (to, for) extreme hunger.

> **Master Student Tip**   **Word Families**
>
> Word families include the words formed by adding a prefix to one of the word forms, as well as those formed by adding a suffix. For example, *migrate*, *migration*, and *immigration* are all part of the same word family and have related meanings.

EXERCISE 6 Use a dictionary and your knowledge of suffixes and prefixes to complete the word family chart. Compare your word families with another student's. Then complete the sentences with the correct forms of the words. The first one has been done for you as an example.

Noun (person)	Noun	Verb	Adjective	un-
—			global	—
	migration			—
—	motivation			
respondent	response	respond	responsive	unresponsive
		survive	—	—

1. " _Survival_ of the fittest" refers to the ability of some animals to live while others die in a given set of conditions.

2. The _____ patterns of animals are generally in a north-south direction.

3. A _____ in our classroom shows the topography, or surface features, of Earth.

4. Because the work is seasonal, not permanent, the harvesting of fruits and vegetables is often done by _____.

5. Have you _____ to the invitation?

6. The company hired a _____ speaker to help improve the performance of its employees.

7. His _____ to succeed came from his desire to escape poverty.

8. Although the doctor tried many treatments, the patient remained _____.

Section 2

EXERCISE 7 Look at Word List 4.2 and the example sentences. Put a check mark in the box next to each word you already know. Leave the third column blank for now.

WORD LIST 4.2

Know it?	Word	POS	Example
☐	**bulk**	*n.*	The people seemed tiny against the **bulk** of the ship.
☐	**generation**		The initial move can be a real hardship for immigrants, but the hope of a better life for the next **generation** motivates them.
☐	**network**		Migration generally occurs through established **networks** of routes and connections.
☐	**range**		Farm workers follow the seasonal harvests in much the same way that migratory animals have a seasonal **range** of movement.
☐	**restricted**		There is a **restricted** zone along the border. The government **restricted** the number of immigrants allowed into the United States.
☐	**decade**		During the last four **decades**, armed conflicts in central Africa have created waves of refugees.
☐	**neutral**		In times of war, **neutral** countries attract many refugees.

EXERCISE 8   Use a dictionary to find the definitions. Then make flash cards to study the words in Word List 4.2.

> **Master Student Tip**   **Parts of Speech**
>
> Although you may recognize the *-ed* form of a word as a verb, it can function like an adjective. The past participles of irregular verbs can function as adjectives too. For example, we refer to *the spoken word* and to *cooked vegetables*.

EXERCISE 9   Study the example sentences in Word List 4.2. Try to guess the part of speech for each vocabulary word. Then, using a dictionary, fill in the third column with the part of speech. Add the part of speech to your flash cards. The first part of speech has been provided for you as an example.

EXERCISE 10   Answer the following questions:

1. In which **decade** were you born? _____

2. What kinds of things might you buy in **bulk**?

   _____

3. In what academic contexts can you use the word **network**?

   _____

4. How many **generations** of one family typically live together in your culture?

   _____

5. Name a **neutral** color. _____

6. What is the typical **range** of temperatures during the year where you live?

   _____

7. Name some things that can be **restricted**.

   _____

EXERCISE 11 Complete each sentence with a word from Word List 4.2. You may need to change the word form slightly. The first one has been done for you as an example.

1. Switzerland is a _____*neutral*_____ country; it has not fought in a war since the sixteenth century.

2. The 1960s were a _____ of social change.

3. The baggage area of the airport was _____ ; only authorized personnel could enter it.

4. Maria's family has lived in Arizona for many _____. Her ancestors settled there in the early 1800s.

5. People often move from rural areas to cities because of the greater _____ of jobs available in urban areas.

6. Immigrants sometimes find their first jobs and places to stay through a _____ of family and community contacts.

7. Although Mexican migration to the United States occurred throughout the twentieth century, the _____ of this migration took place between 1961 and 1990.

8. A _____ of highways crisscrosses the country.

9. Their family has fourteen people, so they buy everything in _____.

EXERCISE 12 The prefixes *deca-* and *deci-* mean "ten." Thus, a *decade* is "ten years." How many other words that begin with *deca-* or *deci-* can you think of? Write them on the lines below.

_____

_____

Can you think of any other prefixes that indicate a number?

_____

_____

Section 3

EXERCISE 13 Look at Word List 4.3 and the example sentences. Put a check mark in the box next to each word you already know. Leave the third column blank for now.

WORD LIST 4.3

Know it?	Word	POS	Example
☐	comment		The professor's **comments** are based on his field research. "Can you **comment** on the situation?" asked the interviewer.
☐	lecture		The sociology class is based on the textbook and the professor's **lectures**. He **lectured** for an hour.
☐	paragraph		The first line of a **paragraph** is indented.
☐	scope		What is the **scope** of the problem?
☐	significant		The wars in Central Africa have had a **significant** impact on human migration patterns.
☐	survey		Sociologists use **surveys** and interviews to gather data. He **surveyed** the city from the hilltop.
☐	topic		Human migration is a **topic** of interest to him.
☐	trend		What **trends** in migration do we observe today?

EXERCISE 14 Read and discuss the following passage about sociology. With a partner, figure out the meaning of the bold words and their part of speech. Check your guesses by looking up the words in a dictionary. Then fill in the third column in Word List 4.3 and make flash cards to study the words.

SOCIOLOGY

Sociology is the study of society and the way it is organized. A sociology course in college is usually based on the instructor's **lectures**, but it may also involve some field research. A sociologist uses tools such as **surveys**, interviews, and observation to research a **topic**. A **survey** is a useful tool, because it generally uses a numerical scale to evaluate something rather than asks for an individual's **comments**. Even when there is a space for them, the **comments** are usually no longer than a **paragraph**. When the numerical data are graphed, it is easy to see upward or downward **trends**. Statistical analysis can also be used on the data to determine if the results are **significant**. By studying these patterns, a sociologist can determine the **scope** of a problem.

EXERCISE 15 Match the sentence halves, and then write the sentences on a sheet of paper. The first one has been done for you as an example.

1. ___d___ There are generally six to eight sentences

2. _____ Dr. Smith gave a **lecture**

3. _____ Her **comments** helped

4. _____ Migration has a **significant**

5. _____ As more women become educated, there is a **trend**

6. _____ At dinner, the **topic**

7. _____ Most students are required to

8. _____ The guerrillas have increased

a. me revise my paper.
b. impact on culture.
c. of conversation was **global** culture.
d. in a good **paragraph**.
e. take a **survey** of world history.
f. the **scope** of their activities.
g. toward smaller families.
h. on human geography.

EXERCISE 16 Match the vocabulary word in column A with its synonym in column B. You will not use all the possible synonyms.

A	B
1. _____ comment	a. overview
2. _____ significant	b. subject
3. _____ topic	c. range
4. _____ survey	d. important
5. _____ trend	e. analysis
6. _____ scope	f. pattern
	g. remark

EXERCISE 17 Answer the following questions about the words in Word List 4.3.

1. Which three words can be a noun and a verb? _____

   _____

2. Which word can also be a suffix meaning "an instrument for viewing"?

   _____

3. Which word contains the suffix -*graph*, meaning "something written

   or drawn"? _____

4. Which two words contain only one syllable? _____

   _____

5. Which word means "important"? _____

6. Which word often follows the adjectives *upward* and *downward*?

   _____

7. Which word has four syllables? _____

Section 4

CHAPTER 4 REVIEW

EXERCISE 18 Before continuing with the review exercises, use your flash cards to test yourself on the vocabulary words from Chapter 4.

EXERCISE 19 Group all the words in the chapter by their pronunciation patterns. One word has been done for you as an example.

bulk	lecture	paragraph	significant
comment	migration	principal	survey
decade	motivation	range	survive
estate	network	response	topic
generation	neutral	restricted	trend
global	overseas	scope	

1-1	
2-1	
2-2	
3-1	
3-2	
3-3	
4-2	*significant*
4-3	

EXERCISE 20 Write the letter of the word that best completes each sentence. The first one has been done for you as an example.

1. ___a___ The Peace Corps sends many American volunteers to work _____.
   a. overseas   **b.** estate

2. _____ Your essay must have an introductory _____ and a conclusion.
   a. topic   **b.** paragraph

3. _____ The Roaring Twenties was a _____ of change for women in the United States.
   a. generation   **b.** decade

4. _____ Immigrants have made a _____ contribution to American history.
   a. significant   **b.** scope

5. _____ What was the _____ for the crime?
   a. comment   **b.** motivation

6. _____ Economists analyze market _____.
   a. trends   **b.** lectures

7. _____ These funds are _____; they can only be used to purchase computers.
   a. bulk   **b.** restricted

8. _____ The college did a _____ of all sophomores to determine their level of satisfaction with student services.
   a. range   **b.** survey

9. _____ There will be a meeting of _____ trade representatives to discuss the General Agreement on Trade and Tariffs (GATT).
   a. global   **b.** migration

10. _____ "Man cannot _____ by bread alone" is a famous quotation.
    a. respond   **b.** survive

11. _____ Hydroelectric plants are the _____ source of electricity in Canada.
    a. neutral   **b.** principal

12. _____ All the computers in the lab at the college are part of the same _____.
    a. network   **b.** range

W E B P O W E R

You will find additional exercises related to the content in this chapter at **elt.heinle.com/collegevocab**.

The Science of Food

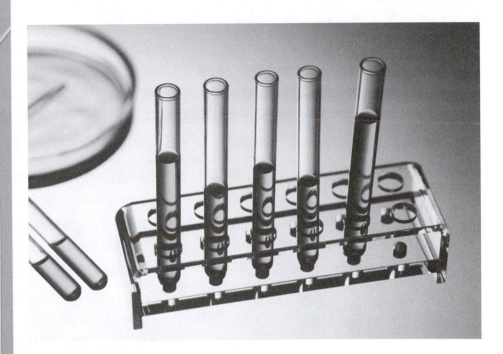

In this chapter, you will

- ► Become familiar with twenty-three new academic vocabulary words
- ► Review **suffixes**
- ► Learn new **prefixes**
- ► Practice using a **dictionary** effectively
- ► Become familiar with science vocabulary

Section 1

EXERCISE **1** Look at Word List 5.1. Put a check mark in the box next to each word you know already. Leave the third column blank for now. (The chart heading POS stands for "part of speech.")

WORD LIST 5.1

Know it?	Word	POS	Example
☐	accurate	*adj.*	**Accurate** measurement is important in making bread.
☐	adequate		The heat must be **adequate** for the yeast to react.
☐	chemical		The **chemical** symbol for salt is NaCl.
☐	expansion		*Rising* is the **expansion** of the bread dough caused by air bubbles.
☐	interaction		The **interaction** of baking soda and vinegar can also be used to make bread rise.
☐	reaction		A chemical **reaction** causes bread to rise.
☐	symbolic		Bread is used in many **symbolic** ways.
☐	visible		Bubbles **visible** on the surface of bread dough show that the yeast is active.

EXERCISE **2** Use your knowledge of suffixes and a dictionary to fill in the part of speech (noun, adjective, adverb, verb) in the third column of Word List 5.1. The first one has been done for you as an example. What can you say about the following suffixes? Which part of speech do they often indicate?

-ate _____ADJ_____   *-ic* _____

-ible _____   *-sion* _____

-tion _____   *-al* _____

EXERCISE 3 Use a dictionary to find definitions of the bold words in Word List 5.1. Then make flash cards to study the words.

EXERCISE 4 Is each of the following statements true or false? Circle the correct answer. If the statement is false, correct it.

1. True / False   An atom is **visible** to the naked eye.

2. True / False   **Expansion** means to grow smaller.

3. True / False   The dove is **symbolic** of peace.

4. True / False   Water is a **chemical** compound.

5. True / False   If you count the number of paces you take to cross a room, you will get an **accurate** measurement of the room.

6. True / False   Four hours of sleep is **adequate** each night for good health.

7. (True) / False   The **interaction** of vinegar and baking soda produces bubbles.

8. True / False   Laughing is a typical **reaction** to pain.

EXERCISE 5   Complete the word family chart below. Use a dictionary to check the different forms of the words.

Verb	Noun	Adjective	Adverb
interact	*interaction*	*interactive*	*interactively*
	reaction		—
—		adequate	
		symbolic	
—		chemical	
—		accurate	
	expansion		—
—		visible	

Now complete the following sentences by writing the appropriate word from each word family.

1. Bread _____ "life" in some cultures.

2. As the bubbles rise and _____ with the heat, the bread rises.

3. When using baking powder, the success of the bread depends on having an _____ amount of baking powder for the quantity of flour used.

4. _____ additives are often put into processed food to preserve it.

5. You must measure _____.

6. Some fruits deepen in color as they become riper; however, others have no _____ change.

7. Can you describe the _____ of the yeast and sugar in making bread?

8. Yeast does not interact with the sugar in the way a chemical _____ to another chemical; it consumes the sugar, giving off carbon dioxide and alcohol.

Master Student Tip   **Prefixes**

One of the most important groups of **prefixes** to learn is the group of prefixes that means "not." For example, if we compare *impossible* and *possible*, we see that the prefix *im-* means "not." Other prefixes in this group are *in-*, *dis-*, *non-*, and *un-*.

EXERCISE 6   Use a dictionary to answer the following questions:

1. Which prefix would you add to create words with the following meanings?

   _____ visible: not visible

   _____ adequate: not adequate.

   _____ accurate: not accurate.

2. In the word ***interaction***, does the *in-* at the beginning mean "not"?

3. Compare the following words and their definitions. See if you can break them into the appropriate **prefixes**, **suffixes**, and **word stems**.

		Prefix	Stem	Suffix
reaction	a response to something	———	———	———
interaction	to act on or affect each other	———	———	———
action	a completed act	X	ACT	ion
inaction	a lack or absence of action	———	———	———

4. What do the following prefixes mean? List as many words as you can that begin with each of these prefixes. Then compare your list with other students' lists. If you are unsure of the spelling, consult a dictionary.

re- _____   *inter-* _____   *in-* _____

_____   _____   _____

_____   _____   _____

_____   _____   _____

_____   _____   _____

_____   _____   _____

5. How many words can you think of that begin with one of the other "not" prefixes?

dis- _____   *non-* _____   *un-* _____

_____   _____   _____

_____   _____   _____

_____   _____   _____

_____   _____   _____

Section 2

EXERCISE **7** Look at Word List 5.2. Put a check mark in the box next to each word you know already. Leave the third column blank for now.

WORD LIST 5.2			
Know it?	**Word**	**POS**	**Example**
☐	bond	*n.*	In polyunsaturated fats, the carbon atoms are joined by a double **bond**.
☐	deduction		The cook's **deductions** about the failure of the recipe were based on her knowledge of chemistry.
☐	index		Look up the recipe in the **index** of the cookbook.
☐	internal		Chicken should be cooked to an **internal** temperature of 190°F.
☐	output		New plant varieties and agrochemicals have increased the food **output** from a given plot of land.
☐	technology		**Technology** has changed the way we grow and preserve food.
☐	transformation		Acid causes the **transformation** of green vegetables into brown when they are cooked.

EXERCISE 8 Study the example sentences in Word List 5.2. Use a dictionary to help you determine the part of speech of each word. Then fill in the third column in the chart. The first one has been done for you as an example. Make flash cards to study the words, using a dictionary to check meanings. Remember that sometimes a word can be more than one part of speech, so note that information on your flash card for those words.

Master Student Tip   **Dictionary Use**

When using a dictionary to look up a word, always read the entire entry and study the examples. Studying the examples can help you choose the appropriate collocations in your own writing. If you look up a word when you are reading, you may need to read the entire entry to find the definition that best fits that context.

EXERCISE 9 Study the following three definitions for the word *deduction.* Then, on the line, write the number of the meaning being used in each of the sentences.

Deduction

1. An amount that is deducted or taken away
2. The process of reaching a conclusion by reasoning
3. A conclusion reached by this process

   a. _____ In addition to taxes, retirement, and insurance, each month I have a **deduction** for my dependent care account taken from my paycheck.

   b. _____ Your **deductions** proved true; you guessed the identity of the murderer.

   c. _____ How many **deductions** should I claim when filing my taxes?

   d. _____ Although several theories try to explain why the dinosaurs became extinct, not all of them are based on scientific **deduction**.

> **Master Student Tip**   **Interference**
>
> Sometimes when you try to learn words that are similar in meaning or spelling, **interference** occurs. Words such as *confirm* and *confer* are not similar in meaning, but they are similar in spelling You may confuse the words because they are too much alike. It is better not to learn similar words together. In the future, when you are creating your own study lists, put these similar words in separate groups to study them.

EXERCISE 10 The following prefixes are commonly used in English. Compare their meanings with the definitions you wrote on your flash cards for the words from Word List 5.2. Do these prefixes help you remember the definitions of the words? Where possible, write your own definition for the vocabulary word. Base each definition on the prefix. If a word's meaning is not related to the prefix, leave it blank.

Prefixes

de- out of   example: deform   *trans-* change   example: translate
in- not   example: invisible   *out-* out   example: outside

Words

deduction _____

index _____

internal _____

output _____

transformation _____

Can you think of additional words that begin with these prefixes?

de- _____

out- _____

trans- _____

EXERCISE **11** Match the sentence halves by writing the correct letters on the lines. Then write the sentences on a separate sheet of paper. The first one has been done for you as an example.

1. There is a very strong **bond** _____

2. Sherlock Holmes solves mysteries _____

3. The student **technology** fee pays _____

4. The subject **index** is _____

5. The ugly duckling's **transformation** _____

6. The factory's **output** increased when _____

7. Her **internal** clock wakes her up _____

a. into a swan is a classic children's tale.

b. the old equipment was replaced with a newer model.

c. for equipment and paper in the computer lab.

d. before the alarm goes off.

e. between mother and child.

f. by scientific **deduction**.

g. at the back of the textbook.

EXERCISE **12** Complete each sentence with a word from Word List 5.2. The first one has been done for you as an example.

1. Sugar molecules _____bond_____ proteins together.

2. If you want to know where to find the potato bread recipe, consult the _____ of the cookbook.

3. When green vegetables are cooked, the heat damages the _____ cell walls, causing the color to change.

4. Shirley Corriher's astute _____ about cooking mistakes have made her popular with chefs and test kitchens.

5. The new _____ used in today's appliances can enhance food quality.

6. For cherries, tomatoes, berries, and apples, the _____ in color from green to deep red indicates ripeness.

7. Bovine growth hormone is given to cows to increase their milk _____.

Section 3

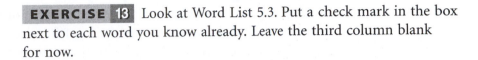

EXERCISE 13 Look at Word List 5.3. Put a check mark in the box next to each word you know already. Leave the third column blank for now.

WORD LIST 5.3

Know it?	Word	POS	Example
☐	attach	v.	A label with the irradiation symbol is **attached** to all irradiated food in the store.
☐	brief		**Brief** irradiation is sometimes used to kill bacteria, insects, and parasites in food.
☐	contact		Bacteria spread through **contact**.
☐	incidence		Proper handling reduces the **incidence** of food-borne illness.
☐	injury		The CDC, Centers for Disease Control and Prevention, promotes health by preventing and controlling disease, **injury**, and disability.
☐	retain		Food **retains** its freshness longer if it is correctly stored.
☐	trace		The CDC **traces** back the progress of a disease to determine its source.
☐	vehicle		Raw meat juices are a **vehicle** for harmful bacteria.

Source: The information in this list is adapted from information on the FDA Food Safety website http://www.cfsan.fda.gov

EXERCISE 14 Use a dictionary to find the definitions, and then make flash cards to study the words in Word List 5.3.

EXERCISE 15 Study the example sentences in Word List 5.3. Use a dictionary to help you determine the part of speech of each word, and then fill in the third column in the Word List 5.3 chart. The first one has been done for you as an example. Remember that sometimes a word can be more than one part of speech. Read the dictionary entry carefully to determine which part of speech is used in the chart's example sentence. Note all the possibilities on your flash card for each word.

EXERCISE 16 Read and discuss the following passage with a partner. Then match the bold vocabulary word with the word or phrase that means the same thing.

FOOD SAFETY

Image of the radura, symbol for irradiation used in labeling food.

The **incidence** of death related to food-borne illness in the United States is 5,000 per year. What many people think of as a **brief** bout of the stomach flu may actually be food-borne illness. To help prevent food contamination, always wash hands and utensils with hot, soapy water before and after they come in **contact** with raw meat. In addition to raw meat juices, egg-rich and cream-based foods can also be **vehicles** for harmful bacteria. The FDA (Food and Drug Administration) and the USDA (U.S. Department of Agriculture) work to protect the public from **injury** by ensuring the quality and safety of the food we eat. Food that is properly handled **retains** its freshness longer. The FDA also requires that nutritional labels be **attached** to all foods. In the event an outbreak of food-borne illness occurs, the CDC (Centers for Disease Control and Prevention) tries to **trace** back the progress of the disease so that the source can be identified.

Source: The information in this passage is adapted from information on the FDA Food Safety website http://www.cfsan.fda.gov

1. _____ incidence
2. _____ brief
3. _____ contact
4. _____ vehicles
5. _____ injury
6. _____ retains
7. _____ attached
8. _____ trace

a. harm
b. cars
c. short
d. touch physically
e. fastened to
f. number of cases
g. carriers
h. follow the trail or path of something
i. keeps

EXERCISE 17   Discuss the following questions with a partner.

1. If you wanted to **contact** someone, what would you do?
2. What does it mean if a food label says that a food contains "**trace** amounts" of a mineral?
3. Name some **contact** sports.
4. What could you use to **attach** two pieces of paper? Two pieces of wood?
5. Have you ever suffered a serious **injury**? Describe what happened.
6. What is the **incidence** of crime near your campus?
7. When you hire someone, sometimes you pay a **retainer's** fee. From the meaning of *retain*, can you guess what a retainer's fee is?
8. An example sentence above states, "Raw meat juices are a **vehicle** for harmful bacteria." A car is also sometimes referred to as a **vehicle**. How are a car and raw meat juices similar?
9. If a message or speech is "**brief** and to the point," what characteristics does it have?

Section 4

CHAPTER 5 REVIEW

EXERCISE 18 Before continuing with the review exercises, use your flash cards to test yourself on the words from Chapter 5.

accurate	contact	interaction	technology
adequate	deduction	internal	trace
attach	expansion	output	transformation
bond	incidence	reaction	vehicle
brief	index	retain	visible
chemical	injury	symbolic	

EXERCISE 19 Group all the words in the chapter by their pronunciation pattern. Say each word aloud to figure out its pattern. Then check your answers with a dictionary. One has been done for you as an example.

1-1	
2-1	
2-2	
3-1	
3-2	
4-2	
4-3	*interaction*

EXERCISE 20 Match each numbered word or phrase with its lettered antonym. Write the letters on the lines. You will not use all the possible antonyms.

1. _____ external
2. _____ contract
3. _____ surplus
4. _____ heal
5. _____ long
6. _____ imprecise
7. _____ input
8. _____ hidden
9. _____ let go
10. _____ stay the same
11. _____ take sides

a. transform
b. injure
c. deduction
d. neutral
e. brief
f. internal
g. retain
h. output
i. expand
j. adequate
k. trace
l. interaction
m. visible
n. accurate

WEB POWER

You will find additional exercises related to the content in this chapter at **elt.heinle.com/collegevocab**.

6

Psychology

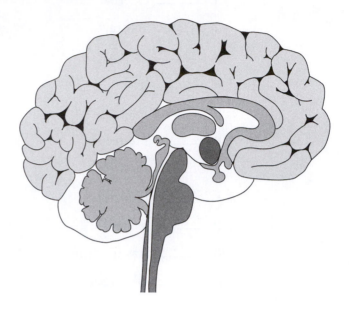

In this chapter, you will

- ► Become familiar with twenty-four **academic** vocabulary words
- ► Work with **collocations**
- ► Learn about **analogies**
- ► Read about **psychology**

Section 1

EXERCISE **1** Look at Word List 6.1 and the example sentences. Put a check mark in the box next to each word you already know. Leave the third column blank for now. (The chart heading POS stands for "part of speech.")

WORD LIST 6.1			
Know it?	Word	POS	Example
☐	psychology	*n.*	**Psychology** is a social science.
☐	academic		College students frequently take psychology as part of their **academic** program.
☐	corresponding		There are aspects of psychology **corresponding** to sociology, biology, and anthropology.
☐	perspective		Psychologists examine issues from a variety of **perspectives**.
☐	objective		Psychologists use **objective** methods of observation and experimentation.
☐	enable		These methods **enable** psychologists to formulate theories about behavior and the way the mind works.
☐	adult		Developmental psychology focuses on the changes that come with age in the development from infant to **adult**.
☐	overall		Although branches specialize in education, each discipline within psychology contributes to our **overall** understanding of teaching and learning.

EXERCISE 2 Use a dictionary to find the definitions of the bold words in Word List 6.1. Then make flash cards to study the words.

EXERCISE 3 Study the example sentences in Word List 6.1. Try to guess the part of speech for each vocabulary word. Then, using a dictionary, fill in the third column of the chart with the part of speech. The first one has been done for you as an example. Add the part of speech to your flash cards.

Master Student Tip   **Analogies**

An **analogy** is a way of expressing the relationship between two pairs of words. It is written in the form **a: b:: c: d**, and is read *a is to b as c is to d*. For example:

physician: medicine:: teacher: education

A physician is a person who is specially trained in medicine, and a teacher is a person who is specially trained in education. Thus, the same relationship exists between *physician* and *medicine* that exists between *teacher* and *education*. Analogies can help you remember the meanings of vocabulary words.

EXERCISE 4 Complete each analogy with a vocabulary word from Word List 6.1.

1. Sociology: society:: _____: mind

2. _____: child:: cat: kitten

3. permit: prohibit:: _____: block

4. period: periodic:: academy: _____

5. injure: harm:: total: _____

6. range: ranging:: correspond: _____

EXERCISE 5   Match the bold vocabulary word with the word or phrase that is related in meaning. You will not use all the related words and phrases.

1. _____ **academic**
2. _____ **adult**
3. _____ **corresponding**
4. _____ **enable**
5. _____ **objective**
6. _____ **overall**
7. _____ **perspective**
8. _____ **psychology**

a. the study of the mind
b. mature
c. total
d. viewpoint
e. unbiased
f. related to school
g. matching closely
h. to make possible
i. above
j. overview

EXERCISE 6   Complete the following paragraph with a vocabulary word or related word form from Word List 6.1.

Psychology is not merely an _____ discipline; it has practical applications as well. Because _____ study human behavior and **mental** processes, their research has applications in health, education, business and law. In the field of health, researchers study certain psychological states and their _____ affects on the body. These studies contribute to our _____ understanding of the mind-body connection, but they also provide a different _____ on illness. For example, research has shown that chronic or extreme stress has an effect on the immune system. Such insights _____ doctors to come up with more effective ways of treating illnesses and chronic health conditions. In addition to investigating the **psychological** side of illnesses in _____, more recently researchers have turned their attention to the psychological and sociological factors that lead to childhood obesity.

Section 2

EXERCISE 7 Look at Word List 6.2 and the example sentences. Put a check mark in the box next to each word you already know. Leave the third column blank for now.

WORD LIST 6.2

Know it?	Word	POS	Example
☐	**implications**	*n.*	Applied psychologists work on the **implications** of basic psychological research for solving practical human problems.
☐	**license**		Most states in the United States require professional counselors and counseling psychologists to have a **license** to practice.
☐	**tapes**		Sometimes psychologists use **tapes** to record what the patient says during analysis.
☐	**classical**		**Classical** psychoanalysis is based on the work of Sigmund Freud.
☐	**rejected**		People **rejected** Freud's theories initially.
☐	**mental**		Freud observed the patient's free flow of thought, or free association, to reveal unconscious **mental** processes.
☐	**nuclear**		One of Freud's best-known theories, the Oedipus complex, is based on the relationships within the **nuclear** family.
☐	**edition**		The first **edition** of Freud's *The Interpretation of Dreams* was published in 1899.

EXERCISE 8 Use a dictionary to find the definitions of the vocabulary words in Word List 6.2. Then make flash cards to study the words.

EXERCISE 9 Study the example sentences in Word List 6.2. Try to guess the part of speech for each vocabulary word. Then, using a dictionary, fill in the third column with the part of speech. The first one is done for you as an example. Add the part of speech to your flash cards.

EXERCISE 10 Working with a partner, see how many collocations you can think of with the following vocabulary words. Write them on the lines. The first one has been done for you as an example.

tape   *audio tape, video tape, tape recorder, masking tape*

license _____

classical _____

mental _____

nuclear _____

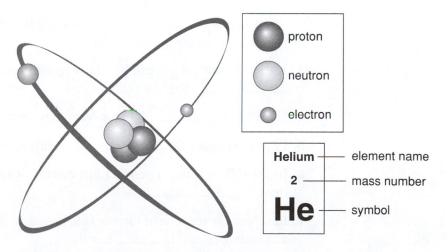

proton

neutron

electron

Helium ——— element name

2 ——— mass number

He ——— symbol

The protons and neutrons together = nucleus

The neutrons and protons together make up the nucleus in an atom.

EXERCISE 11 The word *nuclear* has several meanings. Study the dictionary entry below. Then write the number of the corresponding meaning on the line.

Nuclear

1. relating to a nucleus
2. relating to atomic energy
3. relating to atomic weapons

a. _____ France has many **nuclear** plants that produce electricity.

b. _____ A **nuclear** family is composed of a mother, father, and their children.

c. _____ **Nuclear** proliferation has been a threat to peace since the end of World War II.

d. _____ Weapons of mass destruction include **nuclear**, chemical, and biological weapons.

e. _____ **Nuclear** medicine is used in both the diagnosis and treatment of illness.

EXERCISE 12 Complete each sentence with a word or related word form from Word List 6.2.

1. _____ music has a calming effect on most infants.

2. What are the _____ of changing the physical education requirement in the high schools?

3. Although Carl Jung began by studying with Freud, he later _____ Freud's theories.

4. Which _____ is our psychology textbook, second or third?

5. I need to replace the _____ in my answering machine.

6. In the United States, a person must be at least age sixteen to apply for a driver's _____.

7. Rosalynn Carter, wife of former U.S. President Jimmy Carter, is an advocate for _____ health.

Section 3

EXERCISE 13 Look at Word List 6.3 and the example sentences. Put a check mark in the box next to each word you already know.

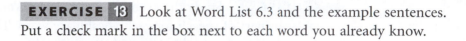

Know it?	Word	POS	Example
☐	**challenge**	*n.*	Psychology has applications for many of the **challenges** facing society today, such as drug abuse and discrimination. Our psychology professor **challenged** us to test our visual perception.
☐	**entities**		Modern psychologists no longer see the mind and body as separate **entities**.
☐	**imply**		Intelligence tests **imply** that intelligence can be measured and given a numerical score.
☐	**marginal**		People who exhibit behavior that is considered **marginal** or abnormal by their society are often diagnosed as mentally ill.
☐	**status**		The **status** of most mental patients improves within six months of beginning treatment.
☐	**styles**		There are different **styles** of psychoanalysis.
☐	**unique**		Psychologists use the term *personality* to refer to that which is **unique** in an individual.
☐	**whereas**		Case studies are used to study individuals, **whereas** surveys are used to study the behavior of groups.

EXERCISE 14 Use a dictionary to find the definitions of the vocabulary words in Word List 6.3. Then make flash cards to study the words.

EXERCISE 15 Study the example sentences in Word List 6.3. Try to guess the part of speech for each vocabulary word. Then, using a dictionary, fill in the third column of the chart with the part of speech. The first one has been done for you as an example. Add the part of speech to your flash cards.

EXERCISE 16 Fill in the blanks with words from Word List 6.3 to complete the paragraph.

The _____ of the child as an object of study and interest is relatively recent. During the Middle Ages, the **status** of women and children in society was _____. In Renaissance art, children are shown acting naturally, _____ prior to that time, they are depicted as miniature adults. During the seventeenth and eighteenth centuries, childhood began to be recognized as a _____ period of development. According to Sigmund Freud, newborns are not aware that they and their mothers are separate _____. His theories _____ that it is the children's experiences that develop their sense of self-awareness. Children learn by facing _____ and learning to overcome them.

EXERCISE 17 *Stylish* and *stylized* are both members of the *style* word family. Both are adjectives, but they are used in very different contexts. Compare the following definitions, and then complete each sentence with the appropriate word. Two have been done for you as examples.

Stylish: very fashionable

Stylized: shown or done in a way that is not natural in order to create an artistic effect

1. The animals and people in ancient Egyptian art do not look natural; they are very _____.

2. Tommy Hilfiger designs very _____ clothes.

3. Frank Lloyd Wright used highly _____ plant images composed entirely of geometric shapes in his designs.

4. The Peking Opera's performance is very ____stylized____.

5. She got a _____ haircut similar to that of her favorite movie star.

6. Tattoos and body piercing are ____stylish____ among many college students today.

7. Monique is a very _____ woman; she always wears the latest fashions.

EXERCISE 18   Answer the following questions about the words in Word List 6.3. Discuss your answers with a partner.

1. Which word in the list is a conjunction? _____

2. What is your marital **status**? _____

3. Which **style** of music or art do you prefer? Why? _____

   _____

4. If someone makes a **marginal** improvement in her or his performance, how much does the person improve? _____

5. Describe a **challenge** you have faced in your life.

   _____

   _____

   _____

6. Which word is a verb? _____

7. Which word can be a verb and a noun? _____

8. Which word contains a question word within it? _____

9. Which words are plural? _____

Section 4

CHAPTER 6 REVIEW

EXERCISE 19 Before continuing with the review exercises, use your flash cards to test yourself on the words from Chapter 6.

academic	enable	mental	rejected
adult	entities	nuclear	status
challenge	implications	objective	styles
classical	imply	overall	tapes
corresponding	license	perspective	unique
edition	marginal	psychology	whereas

EXERCISE 20 Group all the words in the chapter by their pronunciation pattern. Say each word aloud to figure out its pattern. Then check your answers with a dictionary. One answer has been provided as an example.

1-1	
2-1	
2-2	
3-1	
3-2	
3-3	
4-2	
4-3	*corresponding*

EXERCISE 21 Match the antonyms, or opposites. Write the letter of the bold vocabulary word on the line of the numbered word that is its antonym. You will not use all the vocabulary words.

1. _____ modern
2. _____ physical
3. _____ core
4. _____ child
5. _____ accepted
6. _____ common
7. _____ prohibit

a. adult
b. perspective
c. unique
d. academic
e. classical
f. corresponding
g. rejected
h. enable
i. mental
j. objective
k. marginal

WEB POWER

You will find additional exercises related to the content in this chapter at **elt.heinle.com/collegevocab**.